COLONIAL LIFE

A TRUE BOOK

by

Brendan January

Children's Press®
A Division of Grolier Publishing
New York London Hong Kong Sydney
Danbury, Connecticut

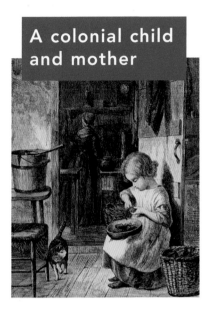

A colonial child and mother

The cover photo shows William Penn negotiating a treaty with American Indians. The title page shows villagers reenacting colonial times in Williamsburg, Virginia.

Library of Congress Cataloging-in-Publication Data

January, Brendan, 1972-
   Colonial Life / by Brendan January.
      p. cm. – (A true book)
   Includes bibliographical references and index.
   Summary: Describes various aspects of life in Colonial America including farming practices, housing, food, medicine, slavery, and recreational activities.
ISBN 0-516-21628-7 (lib. bdg.)   0-516-27194-6 (pbk.)
   1. United States—Social life and customs—To 1775—Juvenile literature. [1. United States—Social life and customs—To 1775.] I. Title. II. Series.
E162 .J36 2000
973.2—dc21   99-058706

Contents

The English arrive in Jamestown hoping to discover riches.

Life in a New Land

In 1607, a ship filled with people from England landed on the coast of the land we now call Virginia. With the permission of King James I of England, they had set out to start a new life in a new land. With axes and spades, they cleared a spot in the forest.

They then built a tiny village of mud huts.

This village became Jamestown—the first successful English settlement, or colony, in North America. Named after King James I, this new village was a colony belonging to England; the people who lived there were called colonists.

The first Jamestown colonists eagerly searched for gold and precious stones in the Virginian countryside. They hoped to

Modern replicas of the type of homes built by the founders of Jamestown.

make an easy fortune and return to England. They never found gold or precious stones.

The Jamestown colonists were the first of many people to come to North America from Europe (the continent

The Pilgrims at a religious service

where England is). Not all of the newcomers wanted to become rich. In 1620, the Pilgrims landed in Massachusetts. The Pilgrims were Puritans, a strict religious group from England. They hoped to create a pure religious community in North America. They started a small village that they named Plymouth. Many more Puritans soon followed the Pilgrims.

In 1682, peaceful Quakers settled in Pennsylvania. They were called Quakers because

A Quaker meeting house

they "quaked" (shook) at their religious meetings. Both groups were poorly treated in England because of their beliefs.

Many colonists came to North America simply searching for a better life. In England, freezing winters had killed crops for several seasons. Food and work had grown scarce. The colonists hoped for more opportunity in North America.

The first newcomers from Europe grew homesick. They

clung to familiar habits and beliefs. The houses they built looked like the ones they had left behind. They cooked and ate food just like the food at home. But soon, the colonists began to eat fruits and vegetables that grew nearby. They built new homes that took advantage of the region's weather. Slowly, the colonists created a new way of living.

The colonists also learned important lessons from people

already living in North America—
the American Indians. Thousands
of American Indians lived in North
America when the first colonists
arrived. Some of the Indians taught
the colonists how to farm and
hunt. Others traded furs, food,
and land to the white colonists. In
exchange, the Indians received
European goods. Indians replaced
their stone axes, clay pots, and
bone needles with metal hatchets
and knives, brass kettles, and
needles of steel.

Colonists and American Indians trade goods

These new tools made Indian life easier. But the Europeans also brought diseases that Indians had never encountered. Thousands of

Many American Indians died from illnesses that were brought over from Europe.

Indians sickened and died. The colonists also took Indian land, pushing the Indians west. After only a hundred years, Indian culture and life on the east coast of North America had nearly disappeared.

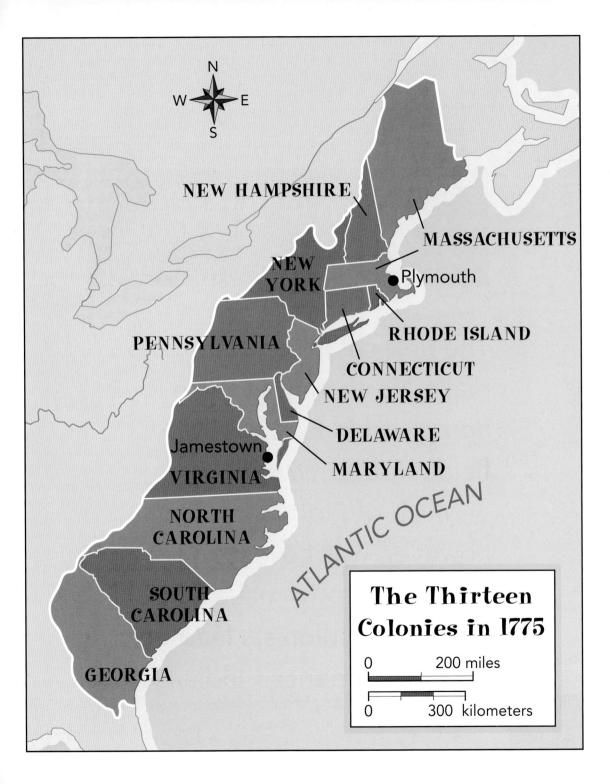

NEW HAMPSHIRE

MASSACHUSETTS

● Plymouth

NEW YORK

RHODE ISLAND

PENNSYLVANIA

CONNECTICUT

NEW JERSEY

DELAWARE

MARYLAND

Jamestown ●

VIRGINIA

NORTH CAROLINA

ATLANTIC OCEAN

SOUTH CAROLINA

GEORGIA

The Thirteen Colonies in 1775

0   200 miles

0   300 kilometers

Farms and Cities

The first colonists wanted to make North America like their homeland in Europe—open fields dotted with villages.

Much of North America, however, was covered with thick forests. To make open space, the colonists learned from the American Indians how

A Pilgrim farmer surveys the land he has cleared to grow crops.

to "girdle" (or strip) trees. The colonist removed a ring of bark from around a tree trunk. Without the bark's protection, the tree soon died. The colonist then planted corn and other crops around the dead tree. Sunlight shone down through the branches. After several years, the colonist cut down the dead trees for firewood, creating an open field.

Behind their homes, the colonial farmers planted vegetable gardens. Nearby, they planted apple or peach trees. To store animals and grain, they built barns. The farmers took their grain to a mill. At the mill, heavy stones ground the grain into flour. Colonists used the flour to make breads and cakes. The

Gristmills use water power to operate the machinery that crushes grain into flour.

flour was sold to nearby neighbors and in the cities.

The cities and towns were filled with merchants and craftsmen—shoemakers, furniture makers, silversmiths, and blacksmiths. In cities along the Atlantic Ocean, ships unloaded

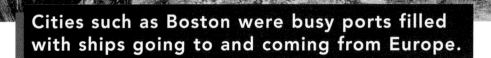

Cities such as Boston were busy ports filled with ships going to and coming from Europe.

goods from Europe, including pots and pans, guns, woven cloth, and spices. By the 1700s, wealthy colonists could order clothing to be made in England and shipped to them in North America.

Houses

The first colonists in North America pitched simple tents. In northern colonies, they bent trees into arcs and tied them together. They covered this structure with straw, grass, and mud. These simple huts were called "English wigwams."

Other colonists dug pits several feet deep. The colonists then lined the pits with tree branches and bark on the inside. Overhead, they placed planks and covered them with thatch (bundles of reeds). These first houses lasted only a few years. The colonists soon replaced them with larger and stronger structures.

In Massachusetts, the Pilgrims and the Puritans built homes much like those in England. The houses were

Pilgrims building houses in Plymouth, Massachusetts

Darley.

made of wood planks, and the roofs were made from thatch. But the winters were long and cold in New England so the colonists learned to make steep roofs from wood. This allowed snow to slide off.

23

A colonial family keeps warm by the fireplace.

Colonists' houses had a giant fireplace to heat the rooms. A fire was kept burning in the fireplace through most of the day, and the chimney quickly became clogged with soot. A broom was used to clean the short chimneys, but for the taller ones, colonists had an odd solution. They would lower a chicken or a goose down the chimney from the top. As it fell, the bird would frantically beat its wings—scrubbing the chimney's walls.

Windows on most houses were small because glass was very expensive. Instead of glass, some colonists used paper soaked in linseed oil (a yellow-ish oil made from flaxseed).

In the southern colonies, the summers were very hot. The colonists built their fire-places at one end of the house to keep the other end cooler. (Most northern homes had a fireplace in the center.) Later, kitchens were built in separate shacks. Southerners also extended their roofs far beyond the walls. This provid-ed more shade from the burning sun.

In Pennsylvania, newcomers from Sweden and Finland

Some log cabins built during colonial times are still standing today, such as this one in Ninety Six, South Carolina.

constructed the first log cabins. These houses were easy and cheap to build. The colonists chopped down trees, stripped off the branches, and stacked the logs on top of each other. Cracks between the walls were sealed with mud and grass.

The Shirley Plantation is one of the many southern mansions built by wealthy landowners.

By the 1700s, the colonists were building houses made from brick and stone. In the south, rich plantation owners constructed giant homes called mansions. Slaves who worked on these plantations lived in shacks next to the fields.

fricans were brought to
e colonies to be slaves.

Slaves were captured in Africa and then taken to North and South America on European ships. The firs slaves arrived in Virginia in 1619. Southern farmers bought slaves to work in obacco fields. The slave population grew rapidly. By 700, one of every five people in the southern colonie as an African-American slave. In South Carolina, lmost half of the people were slaves.

Slaves harvest cotton crops on a Southern plantation.

Slaves held almost o rights. They could narry, but their families ould be broken up. lave owners could vhip their slaves for unishment. The Quakers were the only early

Food

The first colonists were astonished by the amount of wildlife in North America. Every year, schools of fish filled the streams when they swam upriver. One newcomer said that he could cross a stream on the backs of the fish and not get his shoes wet.

During the summer, colonists picked fruit that grew wild, such as black-berries (left) and blueberries (right).

At certain times of the year, flocks of flying birds darkened the sky. Turkeys ran through the forests in herds. Oysters (some more than a foot long) grew in the shallow ocean waters. In the summer, colonists gathered strawberries, blackberries, huck-leberries, and blueberries. In the fall, they ate tasty apples and sweet peaches. They also liked to drink cider made from apples.

Each group of colonists brought food from their homeland in Europe. The Dutch brought cookies (from the Dutch word *koekje*) and crullers (from *krulle*), which were small, sweet twisted cakes. Germans made sauerkraut (meaning "sour cabbage") and coleslaw (from *koolslaa*).

Colonists ate porridge or oat-meal for breakfast and supper. The main meal, called dinner, was

Colonists ate their dinner in the middle of the day.

served between noon and three o'clock. Usually, it was a stew of meat and spices. The colonists also enjoyed fried pork and bacon.

After several years, the colonists' tastes began to change. American Indians introduced them to exciting, tasty new foods.

In Boston, Indians showed colonists how to bake beans in pots. (Boston is still known for baked beans today.) New England colonists also began to eat pumpkins, either sliced or baked into pies.

But the greatest gift from the Indians was maize, or corn. Because it was easy to grow, corn became the major food for the colonists. They pounded corn into powder, soaked it in milk, and ate it for breakfast. They

Corn became an important part of the colonists' diet.

combined corn with beans into a dish called succotash. In the late summer, they ate corn right off the cob. In the south, grits were invented by boiling corn grain into a soft, white mass.

Sweets

One visitor found colonists to be very healthy people, except for their teeth. Like Americans today, the colonists loved

A colonial woman peels apples to make apple dumplings.

sweets. American Indians taught them to tap maple trees for syrup. Colonists also raised bees to make honey. Sugar was bought in large cones. The colonists chipped off pieces to sweeten food. The colonists also satisfied their sweet tooth with cakes, rock candy, and marzipan, an almond-flavored treat made with egg whites and sugar.

Medicine

Most of the first colonists arrived in North America exhausted and weak from their long journeys across the Atlantic Ocean. In the southern colonies, especially Virginia and Maryland, thousands did not survive even one year.

Colonial doctors did not have the medicines that we have

A doctor treats an ill colonist.

today. When colonists suffered from burning fevers, doctors thought that their bodies had too much blood. With a sharp needle, a doctor opened a patient's vein and drained a small amount of blood. This sometimes brought down the fever. But it also weakened the patient and frequently led to death.

Many colonial cures did not work. Some thought that rubbing a pinecone against skin would cure wrinkles. Others believed that eating kidney beans helped the kidneys in the human body.

The colonists learned many cures from American Indians.

Bark from the willow tree was used to stop headaches.

For headaches, the Indians chewed on bark from a willow tree. Today, we know that the bark contains salicylic acid, which is an important ingredient in aspirin.

For Fun

Children and adults both worked very hard in the colonies, but they also made time for fun.

The children played games just like the games today—hide-and-seek, tag, and hopscotch. Older children played checkers, backgammon, and dominoes. The Dutch colonists introduced

Just like today, children in the colonies enjoyed playing games (left). A domino set from colonial times (right).

ice skating and sledding, which was enjoyed by young and old alike.

Adults enjoyed a game called "ninepins," also introduced by the Dutch. On a grassy lawn or street, a player set up nine wooden pins. Players then rolled a ball to knock down as

Adults play an early version of bowling.

many pins as they could. The game became very popular. In Connecticut, some leaders believed that it led to gambling. They banned it. But the colonists outwitted their leaders. They added another pin to the nine and called it bowling. The game is still enjoyed throughout America today.

To Find Out More

Here are some additional resources to help you learn more about colonial life:

 **Books**

Dozier, Susan. **Colonial Cooking.** Children's Press, 1999.

Isaacs, Sally Senzell. **America in the Time of Pocohantas: 1590-1754.** Heinemann Library, 1999.

Knight, James. **The Farm: Life in Colonial Pennsylvania.** Troll Publishing, 1998.

Knight, James. **The Village: Life in Colonial Times.** Troll Publishing, 1998.

McGovern, Ann. **If You Lived in Colonial Times.** Scholastic, 1992.

Warner, John F. **Colonial American Home Life.** Franklin Watts, 1993.

Organizations and Online Sites

Archiving Early America
http://earlyamerica.com/

A site that provides insight into diaries, letters, and newspapers written in colonial America.

Colonial Williamsburg
http://www.history.org/

The homepage for a village that recreates colonial American life.

Colonial Williamsburg Foundation
P. O. Box 1776
Williamsburg, VA
23187-1776

Plimoth Plantation
P.O. Box 1620
Plymouth, MA 02362

Tour of Plimouth Plantation
http://archnet.uconn.edu/ topical/historic/plimoth/ plimoth.html

This site provides a virtual tour of the first English settlement in southern New England.

Virtual Jamestown
http://jefferson.village. virginia.edu/vcdh/ jamestown/

As part of the four-hundred-year anniversary of the founding of Jamestown, this site offers a tour of the village and discusses its importance in history.

Important Words

colony group of people who travel to settle in another land but still obey the laws of their homeland

cruller a fried roll in a twisted or ring shape

girdle to strip a ring of bark from around a tree trunk, thus killing the tree

plantation a giant farm found in the southern colonies where groups of workers—usually slaves— tended the crops

sauerkraut cabbage that has been sliced and soaked in salty water

Index

Meet the Author

Brendan January was born and raised in Pleasantville, New York. He attended Haverford College in Pennsylvania, where he earned his B.A. in History and English. He earned his master's degree at Columbia Graduate School of Journalism. An American history enthusiast, he has written several books for Children's Press, including *The Emancipation Proclamation*, *Fort Sumter*, *The Dred Scott Decision*, *The Lincoln-Douglas Debates*, and *The Assassination of Abraham Lincoln*. Mr. January lives in New Jersey and works as a journalist at *the Philadelphia Inquirer*.